DECADES OF THE
20TH CENTURY

WITHDRAWN

The 1960s

From the Vietnam War to Flower Power

Stephen Feinstein

Enslow Publishers, Inc.

40 Industrial Road   PO Box 38
Box 398   Aldershot
Berkeley Heights, NJ 07922   Hants GU12 6BP
USA   UK
http://www.enslow.com

Library of Congress Cataloging-in-Publication Data

Feinstein, Stephen.
    The 1960s from the Vietnam War to flower power /
Stephen Feinstein.
        p. cm. —(Decades of the 20th century)
    Includes bibliographical references (p.) and index.
    Summary: Traces the events, trends, politics, and important
people of the 1960s, including lifestyles, fashion, arts and
entertainment, sports, environmental issues, and technology.
    ISBN 0-7660-1426-6
    1. Nineteen sixties—Juvenile literature. [1. Nineteen
sixties. 2. United States—History—1961–1969. 3. United
States—Social life and customs—1945–1970.] I. Title.
II. Decades of the twentieth century

D843 .F386 2000
973.92—dc21
                                    99-039424

Printed in the United States of America

10 9 8 7 6 5 4 3 2

To Our Readers:
All Internet addresses in this book were active and appropriate at
the time we went to press. Any comments or suggestions can be
sent by e-mail to Comments@enslow.com or to the address on
the back cover.

Illustration Credits: Archive Photos, pp. 1, 3B, 4, 6, 8, 12, 13,
14, 15, 16, 19T, 19B, 22, 28, 30, 31, 32T, 34, 35, 36, 41T, 43TR,
44T, 44B, 45, 47, 48, 58, 60; Archive Photos/Consolidated News,
pp. 42–43; Archive Photos/Express Newspapers, pp. 16, 17, 38,
39, 46, 52, 60B; Bert Randolph Sugar, *The Great Baseball Players
From McGraw to Mantle* (Mineola, N.Y.: Dover Publications, Inc.,
1997), p. 24; Camera Press Ltd./Archive Photos, p. 61; © Corel
Corporation, p. 56; Douglas or Connie Corry/Archive Photos,
p. 3T; Enslow Publishers, Inc., p. 9; Express News/Archive Photos,
p. 20; Fotos International/Archive Photos, pp. 7, 21T, 21B; Frank
Driggs/Archive Photos, p. 18T; Frank Driggs Collection, p. 18B;
Library of Congress, pp. 10, 23, 26, 32B, 37, 40, 41B, 51, 59;
National Aeronautics and Space Administration, pp. 5, 54, 55,
57, 61B; National Archives, pp. 33, 60; Popperfoto/Archive Photos,
pp. 2T, 11, 17, 29, 60T; Reproduced from the *Dictionary of
American Portraits*, Published by Dover Publications, Inc., in 1967,
p. 61T; Roz Payne/Archive Photos, p. 2B.

Cover Credits: Archive Photos; Bert Randolph Sugar, *The Great
Baseball Players From McGraw to Mantle* (Mineola, N.Y.: Dover
Publications, Inc., 1997); Enslow Publishers, Inc.; John F. Kennedy
Library; Library of Congress; National Aeronautics and Space
Administration; National Archives.

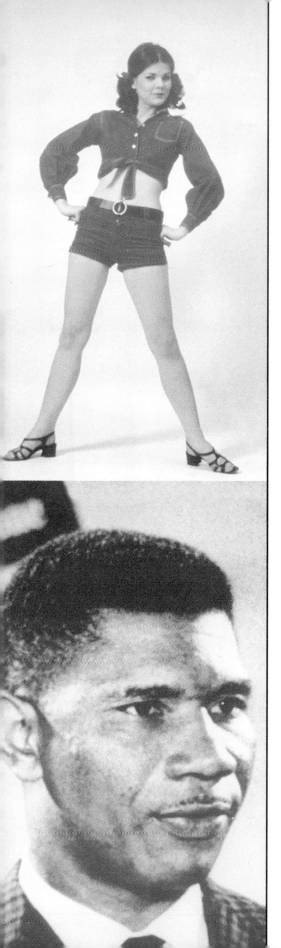

Contents

The 1960s began with a tremendous burst of excitement and optimism. The youthful President John F. Kennedy said that America stood on the edge of a "new frontier" of progress and prosperity. He inspired idealism at his inauguration in 1961 when he said, "Ask not what your country can do for you—ask what you can do for your country." Americans flocked to join the Peace Corps, volunteers who taught people in underdeveloped countries the skills necessary to make a better life for themselves. President Kennedy also set a difficult goal for the nation's space program: to land Americans on the moon by the end of the decade. In 1969, American astronauts did land on the moon and return safely to Earth. Americans greeted this achievement with pride. But the lunar landing was only a temporary distraction. By 1969, the United States was not a happy place.

The decade that had seemed so full of promise back in 1960 would end in confusion, anger, and despair. Political assassinations, a seemingly endless war in Vietnam, violent disagreement over the war, and severe racial tension tore the nation apart.

The 1960s were a time of extreme ups and downs in American life. The enthusiasm inspired by the young President John Kennedy (opposite) as the decade began would be destroyed by the assassination of President Kennedy and other leaders, disagreement over the Vietnam War, and racial tension. Even the successful American moon landing in July 1969 (below) could not dispel the atmosphere of gloom at the end of the decade as Americans looked ahead to continued war in Vietnam and further turmoil at home.

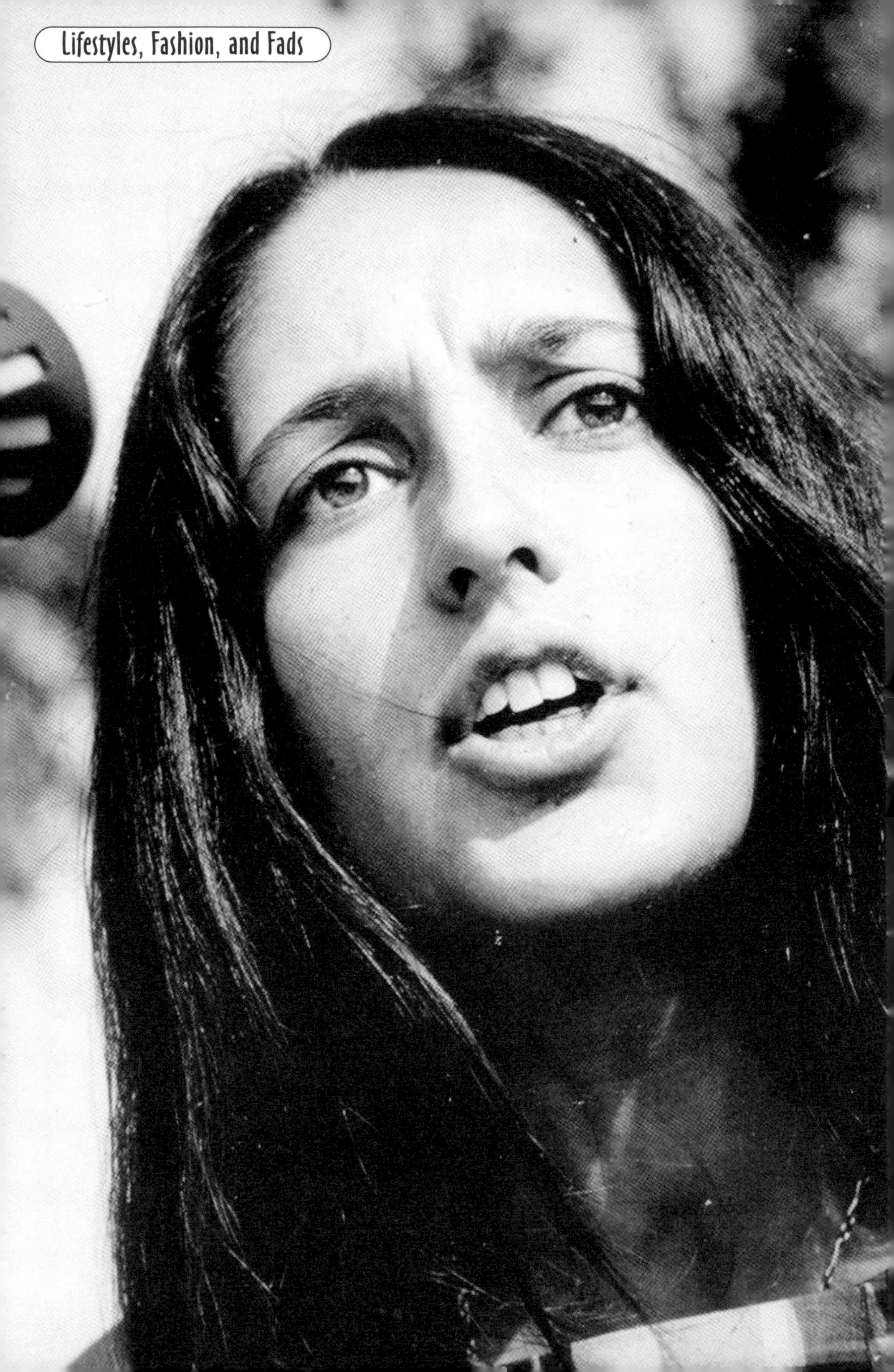

The Woodstock Generation

In August 1969, thousands of young Americans headed for the little town of Bethel in Upstate New York. There, on Max Yasgur's six-hundred-acre dairy farm, they gathered for a three-day event known as the Woodstock Music and Art Fair. Nearly 500,000 people attended this event. They came to hear musicians such as Jimi Hendrix, Janis Joplin, Arlo Guthrie, Joan Baez, and rock groups such as the Who, the Grateful Dead, and the Jefferson Airplane. They also came to be part of a unique gathering of young people.

Many young Americans had begun to question the values the older generations had always believed in. A youthful "counterculture" sprang up to challenge those traditional values. This created a "generation gap" in which young people rejected the beliefs of the older generation and older people considered the lifestyles of the young unacceptable.

Joan Baez (opposite) was one of the best-known and most outspoken folk singers of the 1960s. Her music became very popular among young people, especially those who opposed the war in Vietnam.

Woodstock (below, people play tug of war at the outdoor music festival), with its long list of famous performers and the message of peace expressed by the people who attended, became one of the most memorable events of the 1960s.

7

At Woodstock, a vast crowd of young people—free spirits wearing strange clothes or even no clothes at all—enjoyed the music and each other's company. Some smoked marijuana, some sang and clapped to the music, and some danced. Nobody seemed to mind the rain and the mud. Nobody in 1960 could have predicted such an event as Woodstock and the radically different lifestyle of so many American young people.

The Hippie Lifestyle

Among the crowd gathered at the Woodstock festival were thousands of young Americans known as hippies. They could be identified by their long hair, beaded headbands, tie-dyed shirts, and torn blue jeans. They wore sandals or went barefoot. Actually, many in the crowd were interested in only certain aspects of hippie life. They looked like hippies but still lived a more conventional lifestyle.

The young men and women drawn to the hippie lifestyle, many from middle- and upper-middle-class families, rejected what they considered the shallow materialism of their parents' generation. A life of voluntary poverty seemed better than preparing for a career. In those days of relative prosperity, it was quite easy to live with very little money. Food and housing were so cheap that a person could get by with a minimal amount of work. Hippies often lived in communal situations, sharing rather than acquiring their own possessions.

Clothing came in an amazing variety of styles during the 1960s. Hippies, in particular, made dramatic fashion statements, with their wild hairstyles and "anything goes" outfits (above). From ragged jeans to military fatigues, from miniskirts to bell-bottoms, the 1960s had a fashion for every taste.

Free Love

Hippies believed in free love, preferring to have multiple sexual partners rather than a monogamous relationship. This kind of sexual experimentation became popular with the availability of the birth control pill. Of course, there was a price to pay for "free" love—sexually transmitted disease. There was a dramatic increase in cases of gonorrhea and syphilis.

Drugs and the Counterculture

Hippies used drugs such as marijuana and LSD to "expand their consciousness." People such as Timothy Leary, a former psychology professor, advised young people to "turn on, tune in, and drop out" by using hallucinogenic drugs such as LSD. Many hippies were also drawn to Eastern spiritual traditions. These religions seemed to offer serenity and heightened awareness through meditation and yoga. Gurus from India attracted many followers.

Communal Living

Many communes were established in rural areas. There, hippies could "get in touch with nature." They felt that rural communes offered them an opportunity to live a more natural lifestyle—a mellow, peaceful existence. They could grow their own food, enjoy the beauty of nature, and live in harmony with others. In urban areas, hippie "crash pads" provided places to live for young people who had run away from home.

Many young people of the 1960s, who had come to reject the traditional, conservative values of their parents, looked for ways to express themselves and for new values to embrace. Many experimented with drugs, such as marijuana (below), believing narcotics would free their minds and put them at peace with the world.

The 1960s were marked by severe tensions caused by disagreement among Americans over the Vietnam War. Many young people who opposed the war were very outspoken in their views and held demonstrations (above) to make their voices heard.

The Summer of Love and Flower Power

Hippies came to the nation's attention during the "summer of love" in 1967. That summer, the media was full of reports about young people in bizarre clothing who had appeared in San Francisco's Haight-Ashbury neighborhood, New York City's East Village, and other places. These young people spoke of peace, love, and "flower power." They handed out flowers to strangers, especially people they considered symbols of oppression, such as police officers.

This new counterculture, whose slogan was "Make love, not war," had arisen in reaction to the Vietnam War (being fought to keep Communist North Vietnam from taking over American-backed South Vietnam). Hippies and many other young Americans opposed the war. Not stopping at a rejection of United States war policy, however, hippies dropped out of society to rebel against all authorities and established tradition.

"Too Old to Work, Too Young to Die"

But it was not only the young who went through changes in the 1960s. Older people, too, were creating new lifestyles. How should people live when they are "too old to work, too young to die"? That is what Walter Reuther, head of the United Auto Workers, wondered when he thought about the growing population of retired people. Attention during the 1960s was focused mainly on those under the age of thirty. But people were living longer. While young people engaged in revolution, some older Americans were also pioneering a new lifestyle—as residents of retirement towns.

Retirement towns sprang up in places with a warm, sunny climate—such as Arizona, Florida, and Southern California. People retired to these places to live in peace and quiet. They could pursue activities such as golf, bowling, dancing, pottery, and gardening. Retirement towns even had their own medical centers. Retirement towns seemed to offer everything for a happy and fulfilling retirement. There was only one catch. Nobody under the age of fifty was allowed to live there.

The Mini and the Maxi: A Tale of Two Skirts

Teenage girls were not the only ones to wear miniskirts, the major new fashion of the 1960s. Advertisements told women that they

While some fought to try to end the Vietnam War, others broke fashion rules and started a trend that would sweep the nation. The miniskirt, first introduced by English fashion designer Mary Quant, was part of the Mod Look imported from England. In 1967, Leslie Hornby, an English teenager with a stick-like figure, became the supermodel of the decade known as Twiggy (below).

could look as young as they dressed. Many older women joined the miniskirt crowd, believing the miniskirt held the possibility of eternal youth. By mid-decade, miniskirts were being worn by women of all ages. As the years went by, hemlines crept higher and higher. Some women began wearing the micromini, a skirt that barely covered their undergarments.

To satisfy those who disapproved of bare legs, the maxiskirt, which reached down to the ankle, was introduced. The maxi, however, never gained the popularity of the mini. For those women who wished to avoid the issue of hemlines altogether, pantsuits became a popular alternative.

Although many people thought the miniskirt was outrageous when it first appeared in the United States, it eventually became a staple in the wardrobe of many 1960s women. Even First Lady Jackie Kennedy (below), whose elegant clothing inspired American women to copy her style, eventually wore miniskirts in public.

First Lady Fashions

At the beginning of the decade, American women's taste in fashion was influenced by Jacqueline Kennedy, the First Lady. She wore elegant clothing that was simply designed. American women who could afford it tried to copy her style. Then, the fashion industry discovered a huge new youth market. Before long, styles were being determined by what young people wore. Even Jackie Kennedy appeared in public wearing a miniskirt.

Letting Their Hair Down

In the 1960s, more and more young American men were growing their hair long. Many grew long beards to accompany their long hair. Along with the new hairstyles came the mod look in fashion, which started in England. Young Americans, striving to "do their own thing,"

were eager for anything different. They lined up to buy paisley shirts and velvet trousers. Soon, the mod look was no longer different, and the fad faded. Other fashion fads included the Nehru jacket, the turtleneck, and bell-bottom jeans.

Young men and women of the 1960s also began to adopt a unisex look. Long hair was popular with both sexes, as was secondhand clothing. Both men and women often wore blue jeans, tie-dyed shirts, beads, and sandals. Many women stopped using lipstick and other makeup, preferring a natural look.

Each year, Mattel made new outfits available for Barbie and her boyfriend, Ken (above)—clothing for every occasion imaginable. Each year also brought new improvements to the dolls, such as bendable knees, eyes that opened and closed, and a twist-and-turn waist. In 1968, Barbie was given the power of speech. Also that year, Mattel introduced the Twiggy doll, along with Christie, an African-American doll.

Barbie Dolls

Ruth Handler used to watch her daughter Barbara dressing paper dolls in cutout fashions. One day, an idea occurred to Ruth: What if Barbara could have a real doll to dress—and what if that doll were a teenager instead of a baby? Thus was born the Barbie doll. It helped that Ruth Handler and her husband, Elliot, were toy manufacturers. They sold their first Barbie doll in 1958. The following year, the Mattel toy company presented Barbie at the New York Toy Fair. The rest is history.

Throughout the 1960s, Barbie's popularity kept climbing, as did Mattel's profits. In 1961, Ken was introduced as Barbie's boyfriend. In 1963, freckle-faced Midge, Barbie's friend, appeared. In 1965, Barbie made $97 million for Mattel.

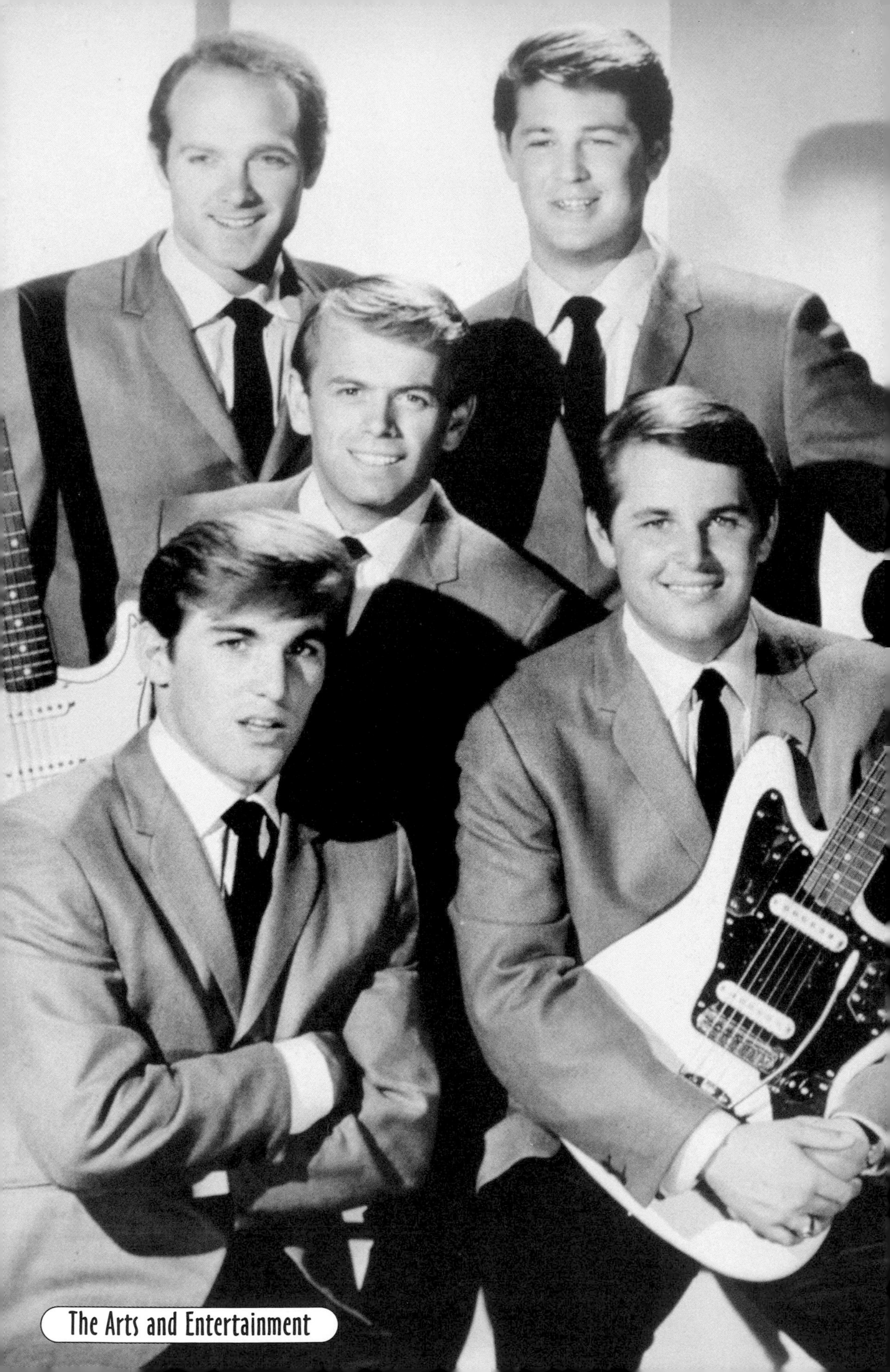

The Endless Summer

The early 1960s was a golden time in the sun for young Americans who listened to the Beach Boys and other surfer rock 'n' roll groups from Southern California. The music conjured up images of the carefree lifestyle of a surfer—the joys of riding the perfect wave, and of partying and dancing on the beach. Helping to promote the beach and surfing fantasy was a series of California beach movies starring Frankie Avalon and Annette Funicello.

It seemed that everyone wanted to surf. Those who lived far from the ocean took up skateboarding. And just about everyone took part in a dance craze that began in 1960 with Chubby Checker's song "The Twist." Dick Clark promoted "The Twist" on his popular TV show *American Bandstand*. The idea was to shimmy and shake, whether on a surfboard, a skateboard, or the dance floor. And twisting was easy—there were no steps to learn and just about anyone could do it.

The upbeat dance tunes of groups like the Beach Boys (opposite) and lyrics that spoke of fun days under the sun were perfect for optimistic Americans of the early 1960s. People enjoyed doing the latest dances, such as Chubby Checker's the Twist (above), which became one of the most memorable dance crazes of all time.

Folk Music

While the beach parties were going on, there were those who marched for peace and joined the struggle for civil rights. Among them were folk singers, such as Joan Baez, Pete Seeger, Judy Collins, and Phil Ochs.

In 1961, Bob Dylan arrived in New York City with his guitar and harmonica. Born Bob Zimmerman, Dylan began singing in coffeehouses in Greenwich Village. Audiences were impressed with the poetry of his lyrics, if not his gravelly voice. In 1963, the folk group

15

Folk performers such as Bob Dylan (above, at left) and Peter, Paul and Mary (above, at right) were very successful in the early 1960s, making records and singing in coffeehouses and clubs. Their lyrics often dealt with the important issues of the day.

The Beatles (opposite) started out as an upbeat rock band loved by teenage girls (opposite, at bottom). Over the years, as they experimented with drugs, they and their "psychedelic" music, with sounds and images that suggested hallucinations, came to represent the ideas of the counterculture.

Peter, Paul and Mary brought Dylan recognition when they recorded his song "Blowin' in the Wind," a powerful statement against war.

The Fab Four

Meanwhile, young people in England were listening to American rhythm and blues and rock 'n' roll—the music of Elvis Presley, Chuck Berry, and Buddy Holly. The Beatles—John Lennon, Paul McCartney, George Harrison, and Ringo Starr—were four working-class lads from Liverpool who loved to play music. They created a unique sound by combining elements of English music with the American rock they loved. When they appeared on Ed Sullivan's television show in 1964, they created a sensation. Teenage girls in the audience went into hysterics, screaming and crying.

Beatlemania swept the country. Young Americans went wild for anything connected to the Beatles—games, wallets, boots, wigs, and movies. Many American musicians began to copy the look and sound of the "Fab Four."

Probably the most successful of these Beatles imitators were the Monkees.

Respect

"*R-E-S-P-E-C-T*, find out what it means to me," cried Aretha Franklin in her powerful hit song "Respect." The message in her song struck a chord with African Americans and with women, who were fighting for respect and equality during the 1960s. Gospel singer Aretha Franklin and other singers, such as Otis Redding and James Brown, were among the most successful performers of black "soul" music. Driven by strong rhythms and expressing powerful emotion, soul music grew from a combination of gospel music and rhythm and blues.

Motown, another popular style of black music in the 1960s, was developed in Detroit, Michigan, by record producer Berry Gordy, Jr. He toned down the raw emotion of soul and added slick arrangements to appeal to whites as well as blacks. His plan worked. During the mid- and late-1960s, Motown was America's favorite dance music. Among the most successful Motown artists were the Supremes, the Temptations, Martha and the Vandellas, Stevie Wonder, and Marvin Gaye.

Black soul music, which had long been popular with African-American audiences, found a new following among Americans of all races in the 1960s. The songs of such performers as Aretha Franklin (above) and James Brown (below right) became some of the most popular dance music in the United States.

18

Young people were constantly searching for something new during the 1960s. The world of art was no different. Artists such as Andy Warhol (below) introduced a strange new form of expression called Pop Art (left). In it, ordinary objects, such as stamps and Brillo boxes, became symbols of the commercialism of American middle-class consumers.

Pop Art

In a decade in which every tradition was questioned, some artists, bored with earlier styles, tried to create new styles of painting. Andy Warhol's paintings of consumer items such as Campbell's soup cans, Roy Lichtenstein's paintings of comic-book illustrations, and Jasper Johns's painting of an American flag taught people to see the familiar in a new way. This type of art came to be called Pop Art, because of its popular subject matter. Andy Warhol also made experimental films. One of them showed the Empire State

Audiences loved Hair *(above) because of the youthful energy expressed in the choreography and music, especially in songs such as "Aquarius" and "Let the Sun Shine In." It was also popular among young people, who could relate to the themes of draft-dodging and drug use discussed in the play.*

Building for twenty-four hours straight. Another style of painting, known as Op Art, consisted of geometric patterns of lines and waves that created optical illusions of movement. Art lovers were often seen rubbing their eyes after viewing such paintings.

Hair on Broadway

In the late 1960s, theatergoers on Broadway were treated to a play about a young American draftee who meets a group of hippies in Central Park while on his way to fight in Vietnam. *Hair*, as the play was called, used all the major themes and conflicts of the day—the antiwar movement, marijuana smoking, free love, the generation gap, and of course, hair—long hair.

On the Big Screen, on the Little Screen

"Plastics" was the single word of career advice given to Dustin Hoffman, a young college grad in the 1967 movie *The Graduate*. Young audiences related to Hoffman's character's confusion about career choice—or whether even to have a career—and his confusion about sexuality and relationships. The 1969 movie *Easy Rider* also appealed to young audiences, who identified with the countercultural lifestyles and values it portrayed.

In 1968, moviegoers lined up to see *2001: A Space Odyssey*, director Stanley Kubrick's film about manned space exploration, artificial intelligence, and the place of human beings in the universe. In one memorable sequence, the film compresses millions of years of human evolution into an instant: A bone tossed by a prehistoric ape-man whirls about in the air and seems to be transformed into a spaceship slowly spinning in space.

Science fiction showed up on the little screen, too, in the form of a TV series known as *Star Trek*, about space voyagers boldly going "where no man has gone before."

The sometimes confused lifestyles of the 1960s were summed up in the films of the day. Dustin Hoffman's role in The Graduate (above) and Peter Fonda's character in Easy Rider (below) reminded many young people of their own searches for direction and attempts to gain self-awareness.

When *Star Trek* premiered in 1966, audiences seemed uninterested. The program never did well in the ratings during its three-year network run. However, years later, after it went into syndication, *Star Trek* and its offshoot series, such as *Star Trek: The Next Generation* and *Deep Space Nine*, developed a cult following, becoming some of the more popular shows on television.

TV Generation

The 1960s were the first decade in which television played a very important role in American life. In the presidential election of 1960, the televised debates between Republican candidate Richard Nixon and Democratic candidate John F. Kennedy were considered a turning point. The handsome, youthful Kennedy, who looked tan and fit on TV, won the election. By the late 1960s, television would be a major part of another big issue—the Vietnam War. For the first time in history, Americans were able to watch nightly broadcasts detailing the progress of the war. They saw firsthand how many people were being killed every day. Television became more than a means of entertainment. It helped change the minds of many Americans about the war in Vietnam.

Although at the time it first premiered, Star Trek (cast opposite) was not very popular among American audiences, it became a favorite when it went into reruns. The original show, starring William Shatner as the stoic Captain Kirk and Leonard Nimoy as the intelligent, pointy-eared Mr. Spock, inspired several later spin-off series.

Television was a big part of the lives of Americans during the 1960s. From daily coverage of the war in Vietnam to sitcoms and game shows, television had an impact in many ways. In fact, many believed that the power of television was partly responsible for John F. Kennedy's win in the election of 1960, after a series of televised debates (below).

Shattered Records

L ike most other aspects of life during the 1960s, the sports world was filled with totally unexpected developments. Previous records fell as individuals and teams provided thrills for their fans.

In baseball, Roger Maris of the New York Yankees hit 61 home runs in the 1961 baseball season, breaking Babe Ruth's previous 1927 record of 60. In the 1963 World Series, pitcher Sandy Koufax of the Los Angeles Dodgers struck out a World Series record fifteen hitters in a single game. And he set a new record by pitching a no-hitter in each of the four seasons from 1962 to 1965, with a perfect game in 1965. In basketball, Wilt "the Stilt" Chamberlain of the Philadelphia 76ers scored a record 100 points in a 1962 game against the New York Knicks. And in one of the most amazing record-breaking events of all time, Bob Beamon, in the long-jump event in the 1968 Olympics in Mexico City, jumped 29 feet 2½ inches, breaking the previous record by more than 2½ feet!

Sports in the 1960s were marked by the shattering of several long-standing records. One of these was Roger Maris's breaking of Babe Ruth's record for home runs hit in one season. Maris (opposite) would hold his 61 home run record until 1998, when it was finally broken by both Mark McGwire and Sammy Sosa.

The New York Mets Win the World Series

The year 1969 can best be characterized as the year of surprising upsets. That was the year the New York Mets, baseball's biggest losers, became baseball's biggest winners—by defeating the Baltimore Orioles in the World Series. The Mets, who had become part of the National League in 1962, had performed so poorly throughout the 1960s that they were viewed as a joke. However, in 1969, they came from behind to win the National League pennant, and later, the World Series.

The Jets' "Guaranteed" Super Bowl Win

A few days before Super Bowl III in 1969, the New York Jets were considered the underdog by most football fans, certain to lose to the Baltimore Colts. Jets quarterback Joe Namath loudly disagreed. He said, "We'll win. I guarantee it." And to everyone's astonishment, on Super Bowl Sunday, thanks to Namath's superb passing, the Jets won the game 16 to 7. It was the biggest upset in professional football history.

The Boxer Who Fought Against War

Born Cassius Clay, Muhammad Ali is often considered the greatest boxer of all time. He even referred to himself as "the Greatest." As heavyweight champion in the 1960s, he described his fighting technique with the phrase, "Float like a butterfly, sting like a bee."

But Ali did more than box. In the 1960s, he took a stand against the war in Vietnam. Ali was drafted into the army but was declared unfit for service because he got a low score on an army intelligence test. Many people were outraged by this. They believed that Ali, who was not only a world-famous athlete but also a poet, had to be smart enough to fight in the army. Eventually, the army lowered the minimum score required to pass the intelligence test, and Ali was drafted.

Ali refused to join the army. Not only was he against the Vietnam War, but he was also a Black Muslim. (Black Muslims believed they were a separate nation from the United States and should not have to fight in American wars.) Ali was convicted of draft evasion. His license to box and his championship title were taken away from him. In 1970, however, the United States Supreme Court overturned the ruling. Before long, Ali was back in the ring and was able to regain his title as the heavyweight boxing champion.

Muhammad Ali (opposite) is still considered one of the best athletes of all time. In addition to being a talented boxer who consistently succeeded in winning the heavyweight championship title, Ali was a political activist and an outspoken opponent of the Vietnam War.

The Camelot Era

When Democrat John F. Kennedy became president in 1961, he brought youthful energy and passion to the job. Kennedy had the dynamic personality of a TV star. Americans saw the handsome Kennedy and his beautiful, fashionable wife, Jacqueline, as the height of glamour. They seemed almost to be an American version of a royal family—similar to King Arthur and Lady Guinevere of Camelot, according to some political cartoonists.

Kennedy was eager to shake things up—to "get the country moving again." He personally wanted to shape history. So he surrounded himself with idealistic professors and intellectuals—people who wanted to make a difference. He raised the minimum wage to help American workers, set up the Peace Corps to help poor people around the world, and supported the movement for civil rights.

Crisis in Cuba

In the early 1960s, President Kennedy faced a crisis. Just ninety miles from Florida, the nation of Cuba had been taken over by dictator Fidel Castro. Now Castro seemed to be allying with the

President John F. Kennedy, inaugurated in 1961 (opposite) symbolized the hopes and dreams of many Americans. As the first Catholic president, Kennedy seemed to be a good leader for a nation in which minorities were struggling to win civil rights. Only forty-three when he took office as the second youngest man to become president, Kennedy also appealed to the many young people who were taking an interest in politics and social issues.

One of the first crises faced by the new president was the relationship between Cuban dictator Fidel Castro (below) and the Communist Soviet Union. Americans feared that an alliance between Cuba and the Soviets could lead to the creation of a Communist state just ninety miles from United States territory.

Dr. FIDEL CASTRO

29

Communist Soviet Union. The United States feared communism, believing Communists wanted to take over the world. Having a Communist nation so close to the United States seemed dangerous to many Americans. In April 1961, Kennedy approved an invasion of Cuba at the Bay of Pigs. The invaders—anti-Castro Cuban exiles—were easily defeated by Fidel Castro's forces. Kennedy had been given faulty information by the CIA, regarding the Cuban people's eagerness to topple Castro. The Bay of Pigs fiasco resulted in Castro's becoming a firm ally of the Soviet Union and making the Cuban Communist party the only legal political party in Cuba.

Then, on October 14, 1962, a spy plane flying over Cuba took photos of Soviet nuclear missile bases on the island. Missiles launched from there could easily strike targets in the United States. Kennedy and his advisors had to act. The next two weeks saw a steady buildup of tension between the United States and the Soviet Union. Warnings, demands, and threats flew back and forth between the two superpowers.

On October 22, Kennedy went on television and told the American people about the Soviet missiles in Cuba.

Evidence suggested that the United States' fear of a Cuban alliance with the Soviets was justified. U-2 spy planes took photographs (below) of Soviet nuclear missile bases being built on the island nation of Cuba. This posed a serious threat to the United States. The Kennedy administration became determined to do something about it, sparking the Cuban Missile Crisis, one of the scariest episodes in American history.

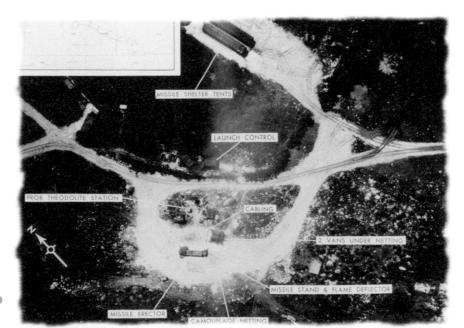

He demanded their removal and announced that American ships would "quarantine," or surround, Cuba to prevent Soviet ships from bringing more missiles to the island. Now the world knew about the crisis and began to fear the worst possible outcome—a nuclear war.

On October 25, Soviet ships neared Cuba but halted at sea. Apparently, Soviet leader Nikita Khrushchev was not eager to start a nuclear war. By October 28, the Cuban Missile Crisis was over. The Soviets agreed to withdraw their missiles from Cuba and dismantle the launch sites. The United States agreed not to invade Cuba.

There were some positive outcomes to the scary episode. Tensions eased for a time between the two superpowers. And a hotline was set up between the American and Soviet leaders so that they could confer instantly in the event of another crisis.

Cuban dictator Fidel Castro (above, at right) eventually made Cuba a Communist country. He also developed an alliance with the Soviet Union and its leader, Nikita Khrushchev (above, at left). For years, the United States has tried to remove Castro from power and eliminate the Communist threat by imposing an economic embargo on Cuba. Over the years, the policy, though unsuccessful, created economic hardship for the Cuban people. Castro remains in power to this day.

Tragedy in Dallas: Kennedy Assassinated

In November 1963, President Kennedy was shot and killed as he rode through Dallas, Texas, in an open car (above, Kennedy at far left) with his wife, Jackie, and Texas Governor John Connally. Lee Harvey Oswald (opposite, at center without hat) was arrested for the assassination. Before he could be tried, he was killed by Jack Ruby (opposite, at lower right with gun). Kennedy's funeral (below) was attended by thousands, as Americans everywhere mourned the loss of their young leader. The tragedy of Kennedy's death destroyed much of the optimism Americans had held during the early years of his administration.

The promising Camelot era came to a tragic end in Dallas, Texas, on November 22, 1963. As President Kennedy and his wife rode in an open car past enthusiastic crowds, gunshots suddenly rang out. President Kennedy was killed, and Texas Governor John Connally was wounded. Within forty-eight hours, Kennedy's suspected assassin, Lee Harvey Oswald, was also shot to death inside a Dallas police station.

Vice President Lyndon B. Johnson (below) became president after Kennedy's assassination. Although LBJ, as Johnson was often called, tried to enact programs to eliminate poverty and to guarantee civil rights for African Americans, he eventually became very unpopular. Many Americans came to blame Johnson for the war in Vietnam. People were frustrated because his administration seemed helpless to either win the war or to remove American troops from Southeast Asia.

The Great Society

Vice President Lyndon B. Johnson became president after Kennedy was assassinated. In his State of the Union message in January 1964, he announced a War on Poverty. And he worked hard to promote progress in civil rights. His efforts led to passage of the 1964 Civil Rights Act and the 1965 Voting Rights Act. These and other legislative measures in the areas of education and medical care were key elements of Johnson's Great Society program. The Great Society was the biggest set of domestic laws since Franklin Roosevelt's New Deal programs of the 1930s. It included programs such as Medicare to provide health care for older people, a Jobs Corps to retrain unemployed workers, Head Start for disadvantaged children, and decent low-rent housing for the urban poor. Johnson's vision for America appealed to voters, who elected him president in 1964. But there was one problem that would use up the billions of dollars needed to fund the Great Society programs and prevent Johnson from turning America into a Great Society.

"Johnson's War"

Since the early days of the Cold War, American policy makers had believed in the Domino Theory—the idea that, if one country fell under Communist control, neighboring countries would also fall. That is how the United States became entangled in the war in Vietnam.

When the Vietnamese won their independence from the French in 1954, the country was divided between the Communists in the north, under the leadership of Ho Chi Minh, and anti-Communists in the south, led by Ngo Dinh Diem. When the Vietcong (Communists in South Vietnam) began fighting the South Vietnamese government in 1960, they received assistance from the North Vietnamese. Meanwhile, the United States had been helping the south by sending economic aid and several hundred military advisors. President Kennedy had increased United States aid to South Vietnam in 1961, sending fifteen thousand military advisors. However, he had refused to send American combat troops to Vietnam.

Lyndon B. Johnson escalated the Vietnam War by sending United States troops to fight. Above, he signs an act granting him additional power to carry out the war.

In August 1964, President Johnson reported North Vietnamese attacks on United States naval vessels in the Gulf of Tonkin, near Vietnam. Congress then passed the Gulf of Tonkin Resolution. It gave Johnson approval to take "all necessary measures" to protect American troops. Johnson now had a free hand to escalate the war. So Johnson planned an intensive bombing campaign. In 1965, the United States took an active combat role in Vietnam. Soon, young American servicemen were fighting and dying in Vietnam. By 1967, there were almost 500,000 United States troops in Vietnam. President Johnson was personally involved in planning war strategy. People began referring to the war in Vietnam as "Johnson's War."

College students were some of the most outspoken opponents of the Vietnam War. By the late 1960s, antiwar demonstrations on college campuses (above) were an almost daily occurrence. Some young people took more radical measures. Many young men, refusing to be drafted into the military to fight a war they disapproved of, burned or destroyed their draft cards (opposite). This illegal action caused many to be arrested. Others fled the United States to Canada or to Europe in order to avoid being drafted.

Campus Radicals

On college campuses across the country, organizations such as Students for a Democratic Society (SDS) organized "sit-in" protests and "teach-ins," marathon lecture-and-debate sessions to educate students about the war in Vietnam. SDS had been formed in the early 1960s by Tom Hayden and several other young people. They felt that students should have a say about university policies that affected them.

In 1964, Mario Savio, a leading spokesperson for students' rights, organized sit-ins at the University of California's Berkeley campus. The university had ruled that students could no longer use a certain stretch of sidewalk as a place to give speeches. Students felt that the university was interfering with their right of free speech. Police were called. Hundreds of students were arrested. But the university eventually gave in to the students' demands.

Within the next few years, students were organizing demonstrations against the war in Vietnam, against military recruitment on campus, and against companies that made war materials. SDS was involved in organizing much of this activity.

By 1969, some members of SDS had become frustrated that peaceful protest had not yet brought about an end to the war. About fifteen hundred of them formed a new group called the Weathermen. Mark Rudd, a former SDS chapter president, joined the new group. He and the other Weathermen felt that violent revolution was the only way to bring about change. They carried out attacks on police stations, courthouses, and banks, using homemade bombs. The leaders of the Weathermen, including Mark Rudd and Bernadine Dohrn, appeared on the FBI's list of Ten Most Wanted Criminals, which was expanded to Fifteen Most Wanted to include them. So they went "underground," where they remained in hiding for many years to avoid capture.

The Civil Rights Movement

Until the success of the civil rights movement in the mid-1960s, African Americans faced discrimination and even violence at the hands of racist whites who wanted to prevent them from enjoying the freedom their ancestors had won in the Civil War. For many years, so-called Jim Crow signs (below) that forced blacks and whites to use separate facilities, from rest rooms to drinking fountains, were a common sight, especially in the American South.

During the early 1960s, civil rights activists were using nonviolent tactics in an attempt to bring about racial justice in America. Most of their activities took place in the South. There, racism against African Americans had long been a part of everyday life. In 1960, civil rights activists staged sit-ins at segregated lunch counters throughout the South.

In 1961, the Congress of Racial Equality (CORE), led by James Farmer, organized a series of Freedom Rides. This was a nonviolent strategy of sending both blacks and whites to places in the South to challenge businesses that practiced racial segregation. The Freedom Riders were often attacked by mobs of angry whites, beaten, and jailed.

In 1962, the United States Supreme Court ordered that James Meredith, an African-American air force veteran, be allowed to register at the University of Mississippi. President Kennedy had to send 5,000 military troops to stop the rioting that broke out when Meredith tried to register, but the university was finally integrated.

In 1963, the Student Nonviolent Coordinating Committee (SNCC) began a program of registering black voters in Mississippi. Freedom Riders set up "freedom schools" in black communities to provide information about voters' rights. The Ku Klux Klan (KKK) and other white racists were enraged. In

WAITING ROOM
FOR COLORED ONLY
→
BY ORDER
POLICE DEPT.

Birmingham, Alabama, in 1963, Dr. Martin Luther King, Jr., and 20,000 other African-American civil rights activists singing "We Shall Overcome" were attacked by the police, who used clubs, electric cattle prods, police dogs, and powerful fire hoses. Many marchers were seriously injured. About twenty-five hundred, including Dr. King, were jailed. In March 1965, King led a march of several hundred Freedom Riders from Selma to Montgomery, Alabama, in another powerful civil rights demonstration.

Black Rage

Martin Luther King had always advocated nonviolence. As the years went by, however, more civil rights activists became victims of racist violence. Among those murdered were National Association for the Advancement of Colored People (NAACP) field secretary Medgar

The Freedom Riders (above) were civil rights activists who tried to end the Jim Crow era by going to public places and entering the areas reserved for members of the white race alone. Often they were thrown out or even attacked, but eventually, most businesses allowed African Americans to use the same facilities as whites. Some areas, however, would require the intervention of the government before they would move to desegregate schools or other public places.

39

Martin Luther King., Jr. (above), was one of the best-known civil rights activists. Respected by whites and blacks alike for his nonviolent tactics and peaceful protests, King became a dominant figure. His work helped lead to passage of such legislation as the Civil Rights Act of 1964 and the Voting Rights Act of 1965. Other civil rights activists were more militant than King. Malcolm X (opposite, at bottom) advocated the creation of a separate nation for African Americans and said that violence might be necessary to achieve racial equality. The tensions of the civil rights era sometimes resulted in violence, rioting, and the arrest of African-American activists (opposite, at top).

Evers, white civil rights demonstrator Viola Liuzzo, and young civil rights workers Michael Schwerner, Andrew Goodman, and James Chaney.

Some blacks began to think that the idea of achieving equality through non-violence was an impossible dream. Many African Americans, especially those who lived in urban ghettos, became impatient with the slow pace of reform.

Black rage finally exploded. In the summer of 1964, riots broke out in Harlem, New York City's African-American community. In 1965, riots took place in Watts, an African-American community in Los Angeles, California. Americans began to dread the summer, when racial riots often took place. Typically, a minor incident involving an African American and the police was all that was needed to set off a riot. Buildings in black ghettos would be set on fire, and people would go on a rampage, looting and destroying property. Police and National Guard troops would be sent in. Often people would be killed in the battles. In the summer of 1967, more than 164 American cities had riots, resulting in 83 deaths, 3,400 injuries, and 18,800 arrests.

Black Power

Against this background of violence, Stokely Carmichael and other black leaders began to think that self-defense was more important than nonviolent protest. Carmichael called for "black power." He hoped to give people racial pride with the slogan, "Black is beautiful." Black activists and intellectuals organized black studies programs at

colleges, where African-American students could learn about African history and culture.

Another black leader, Malcolm X, openly declared, "The day of nonviolent resistance is over." Malcolm X had become a Black Muslim, a group that believed in the separation of the races. He was assassinated in 1965, but others continued to speak up for black power.

In 1967, Huey Newton and Bobby Scale formed the Black Panther party in Oakland, California. Black Panther leader Eldridge Cleaver gave America an angry ultimatum: "total liberty for black people or total destruction for America." The Black Panthers, who never appeared in public without guns, won support from many African Americans. The Black Panthers provided breakfasts for poor black children and conducted street patrols. They also became involved in shoot-outs with police, resulting in many deaths.

Martin Luther King—Tragic Hero of the Civil Rights Movement

As America entered a period of increasing racial violence during the mid-1960s, Dr. Martin Luther King, Jr., continued to organize peaceful protests against racial injustice. In 1964, King won the Nobel Peace Prize. His 1965 voter-registration march in Selma, Alabama, helped bring about the passage of the Voting Rights Act of 1965.

On April 4, 1968, tragedy struck. King was shot and killed in Memphis, Tennessee, where he was lending support to a sanitation strike. The man of peace who had so bravely worked for

In August 1963, Martin Luther King spoke on the steps of the Lincoln Memorial in Washington, D.C., to more than 250,000 people (left). King said, "I have a dream that my four little children will one day live in a nation where they will be judged not by the color of their skin but by the content of their character."

The efforts of King and others eventually helped African Americans achieve equal civil rights and opened doors to new opportunities. In 1967, Thurgood Marshall (above), himself a longtime activist for civil rights, became the first African-American Supreme Court justice.

racial justice became a victim of violence. Once again, black rage exploded throughout America. Rioting in 29 states resulted in 46 deaths, 2,600 injuries, and more than 21,000 arrests.

By the end of the decade, the racial firestorm had pretty much burned itself out. There were some hopeful signs for civil rights reform. Hundreds of African Americans had been elected to public office. In 1967, Thurgood Marshall had become the first black justice on the United States Supreme Court. In 1968, Shirley Chisholm became the first black woman elected to Congress. African Americans began to think that changing the system from within was more practical than violence.

The Election of 1968

As the 1968 presidential election approached, people were disappointed in President Johnson because of the war and the lack of progress toward a "Great Society." The past year had been a tragic time because of the assassinations of Dr. Martin Luther King, Jr., and presidential candidate Robert F. Kennedy, brother of the late president. Johnson was well aware that opposition to his war policies was increasing. He announced that he would not seek re-election as president. Vice President Hubert H. Humphrey won the Democratic nomination, defeating Senator Eugene McCarthy, an outspoken opponent of the war.

But it was Republican Richard Nixon who won the 1968 presidential election. He told voters that he would restore law and order and that he had a plan to end the war in Vietnam. Unfortunately, Americans would continue fighting in Vietnam for another five years, although Nixon did begin to reduce the number of United States troops in the war.

The election of 1968 came at a time when Americans were deeply divided in opinion over the Vietnam War and how best to end it. Politics was no exception. At the 1968 Democratic Convention in Chicago, violence broke out between the police and many of the young people who supported nominee Eugene McCarthy (above). The fighting among members of the Democratic party helped secure the victory of Republican Richard Nixon (right), who told Americans that he had a plan for getting the United States out of the war in Vietnam.

Women's Liberation

In the late 1960s, thousands of women were joining small groups all around the country to discuss such topics as the unequal treatment of women in the workplace and the fact that many men saw women as sex objects. Involvement in these groups inspired many to join or support the National Organization for Women (NOW). The feminist organization founded by Betty Friedan, author of *The Feminine Mystique*, and other women in 1966, fought for women's liberation. The women of NOW believed this could be achieved through better child care, maternity benefits, equal job-training opportunities, abortion rights, and passage of an equal rights amendment to the Constitution. As a symbol of liberation, some women threw their bras in the garbage. Others stopped wearing bras altogether. Many supporters of women's liberation became known as bra burners.

While African Americans struggled throughout the decade to win civil rights, other minorities began efforts to win equal rights as well. Women, in particular, became a force to be reckoned with during the 1960s (above). Led by such women as Betty Friedan, women demonstrated for equal pay, abortion rights, and equal rights under the Constitution. Many feminist activists became known as bra burners, although evidence suggests that very few actually burned their bras.

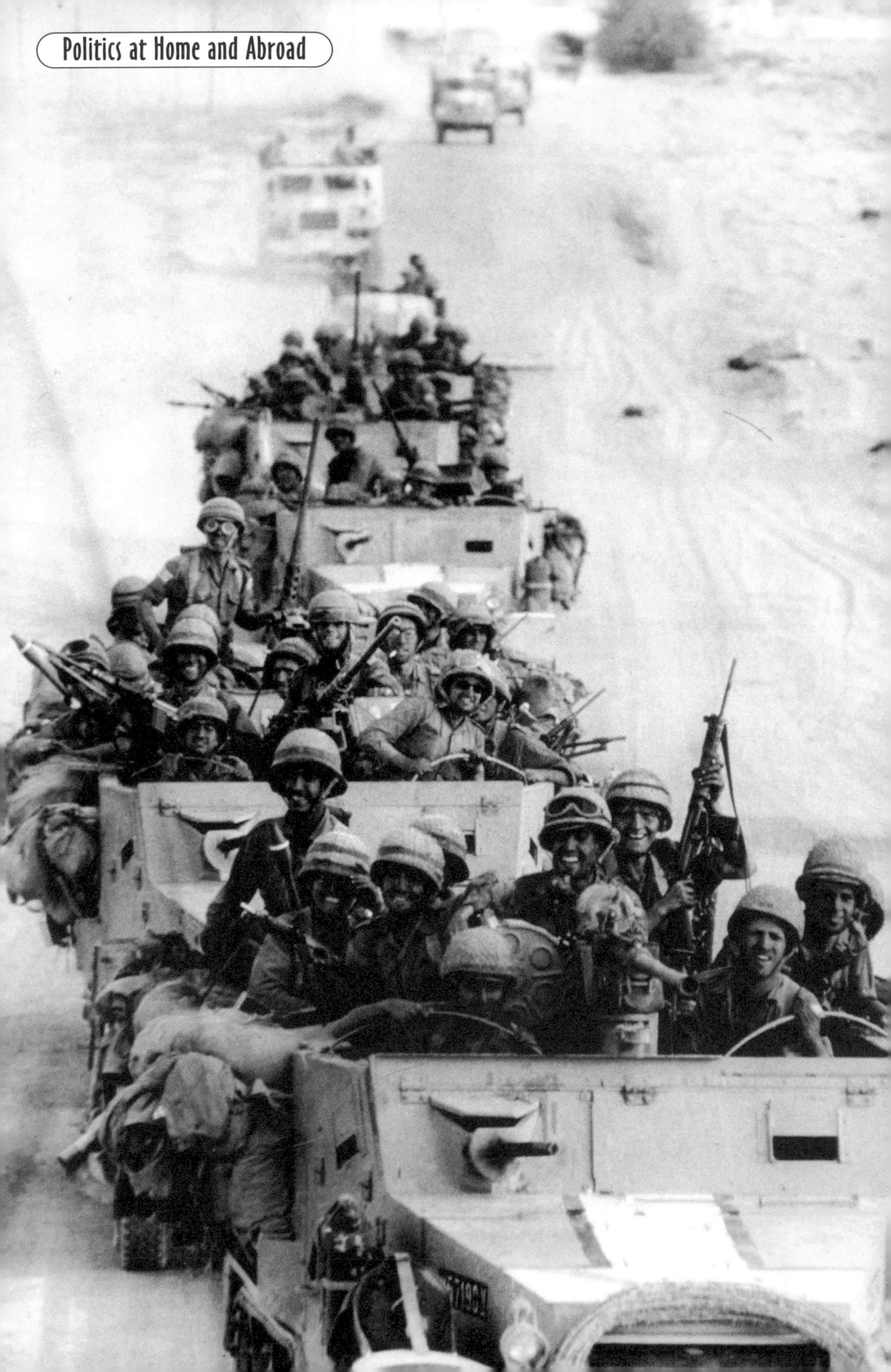

A Chinese Cultural Revolution

The United States was not the only country to experience difficult times in the 1960s. Chinese Communist leader Mao Tse-tung (Mao Zedong) launched a Cultural Revolution in 1966. Its goal was to purge Chinese society of all those suspected of decadent or corrupt behavior, and to make sure that all Chinese remained loyal to the ideals of the Communist Revolution. The Red Guards, consisting of a million Chinese students, were organized to travel about the country and stamp out any trace of traditional Chinese culture or Western influences. Millions of Chinese, especially teachers and intellectuals, were arrested and sent to labor camps. Thousands were put on trial, and many were executed. As many as 400,000 people died.

While Americans struggled with tensions over race and the Vietnam War, other nations faced serious problems, as well. In China, Communist troops under Mao Tse-tung (above) violently attacked their fellow citizens in an effort to eliminate opposition to the Communist regime.

The Six-Day War

On June 5, 1967, the Six-Day War broke out in the Middle East between Israel and its Arab neighbors. Alarmed by war preparations being made by neighboring Arab nations, Israel believed it had to act quickly. With no warning, Israel struck. Israeli planes bombed airfields in Egypt, Syria, and Jordan, destroying the Arab planes on the ground in a matter of minutes. On June 10, the war was over. Israel had dealt the Arabs a humiliating defeat. Israel now occupied Egypt's Sinai Peninsula and Gaza Strip, Jordan's West Bank, Syria's Golan Heights, and the Old City of Jerusalem. The war may have been over for the time being, but tensions would continue for years.

In the Middle East, long a scene of violence between Arabs and Jews over ownership of the Holy Land, war broke out. Fearing an attack by its Arab neighbors, Israel attacked first in the Six-Day War (opposite), bombing Egypt, Syria, and Jordan.

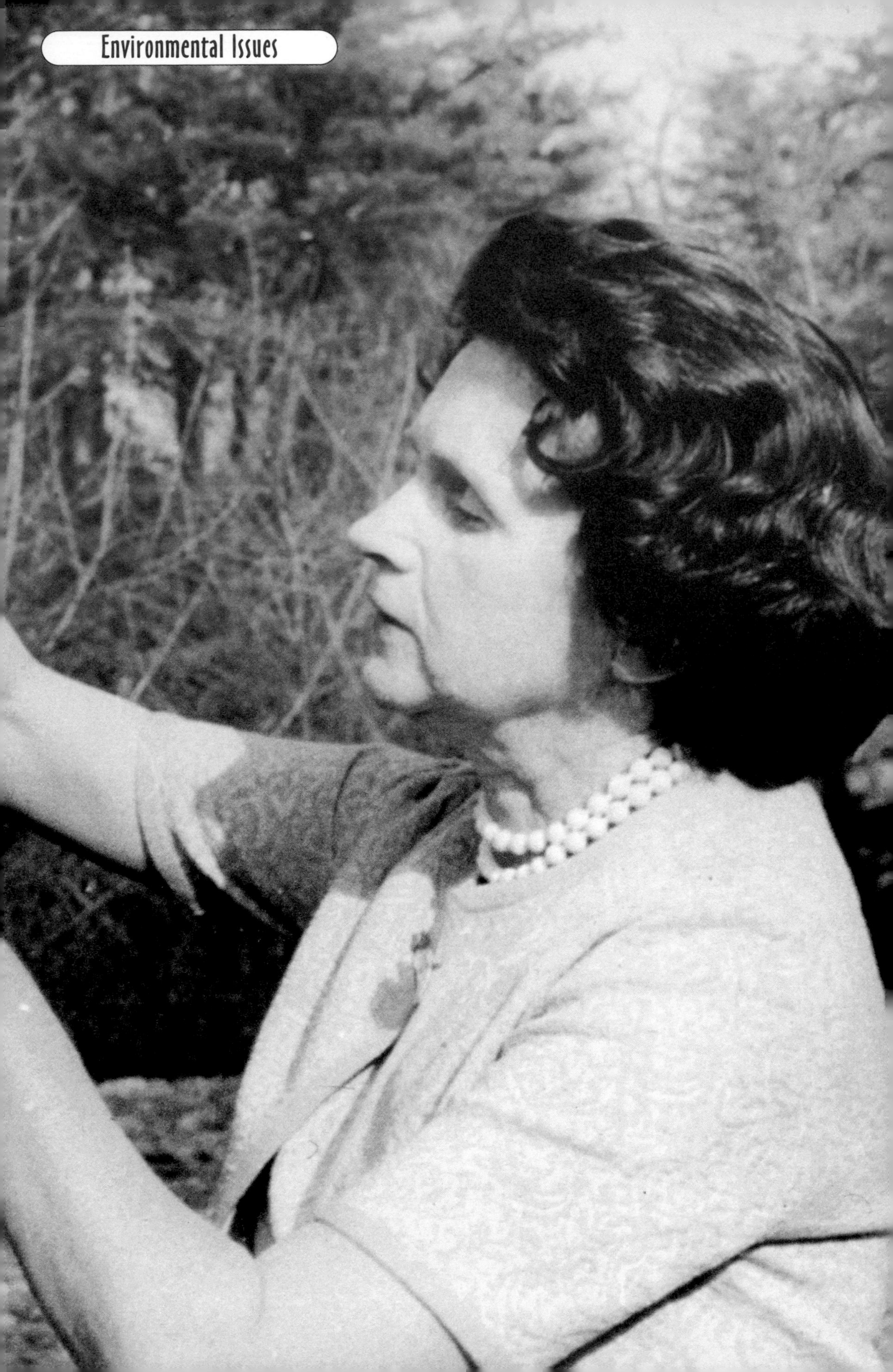

Silent Spring

In 1962, a new book was published that asked readers to imagine a very different world. In this world, there were no birds and no fruit growing on trees. People and animals could drop dead suddenly, without explanation. The author of the book *Silent Spring* was Rachel Carson. She used literature to make Americans aware of the dangerous effects poisons and pesticides used on farms and in homes have on the environment. Carson explained that the terrifying new world she described really existed in parts of the United States and other countries. Her words were very influential. The Kennedy administration confirmed her findings about poison and pesticide. By 1972, the Environmental Protection Agency had banned the use of DDT, one of the most common pesticides.

In the 1960s, few Americans realized the dangers of pollution to the environment. That all changed with the publication of Rachel Carson's book Silent Spring. Carson (opposite) and her book would dramatically affect the attitudes of Americans and help influence the government to set up the Environmental Protection Agency. Carson would also start a wave of environmental awareness and activism that continues to this day.

Controlling Automobile Pollution

The new environmental awareness brought about by Rachel Carson's *Silent Spring* led to other changes. In October 1965, Congress passed an antipollution bill. This new law authorized the secretary of Health, Education and Welfare to establish emission standards for automobiles to prevent air pollution. The law would also ban the sale of any vehicles that did not meet the new government standards.

The new environmental awareness led to dramatic new changes in the law. Realizing that Americans were doing terrible damage to their environment through the use of pesticides and other pollutants every year, Congress passed the Air Quality Act of 1967. Signed into law by President Lyndon Johnson (opposite), it would be one of the first laws to set standards for preventing pollution.

Air Quality Act of 1967

On November 14, 1967, Congress took another big step toward cleaning up and protecting the environment. It passed the Air Quality Act. The law set aside more than $428 million over the following three years to fight air pollution. Congress hoped to prevent the health problems and crop damage caused by automobile emissions and other air pollutants. President Johnson said of the new law, "either we stop poisoning our air or we become a nation of gas masks, groping our way through the dying cities and a wilderness of ghost towns."

Santa Barbara's Disastrous Oil Spill

In February 1969, despite a good start in taking action against pollution, Americans learned they had a long way to go. A huge oil slick in the Santa Barbara Channel, off the coast of California, forced the Santa Barbara harbor to close. The oil slick, more than ten miles long, threatened to harm the area's beaches and wildlife. In response to the crisis, local oil companies agreed to stop drilling for oil in the area until the problem could be brought under control.

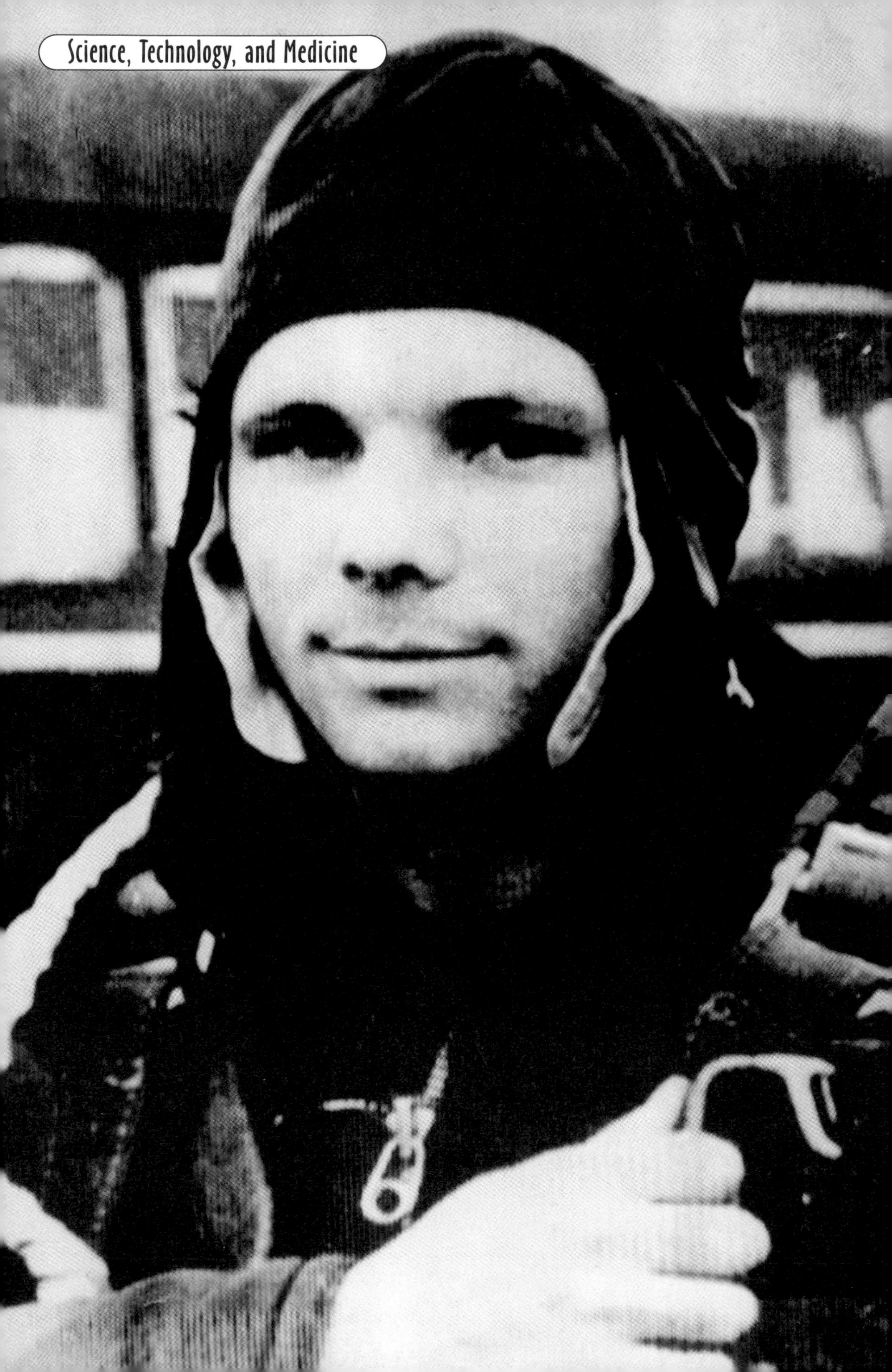

The Space Race

Perhaps if there had not been a Cold War between the United States and the Soviet Union, Americans would never have ventured into space. But from the time the Soviets launched their *Sputnik* satellite into orbit around Earth back in 1957, the United States scrambled to assemble a space program to catch up with the Russians. The race was on!

In April 1961, Soviet cosmonaut Yuri A. Gagarin became the first human being to defy gravity and enter the weightless realm of space. He made one complete orbit of the earth in one hour and forty-eight minutes aboard *Vostok 1*. One month later, United States astronaut Alan B. Shepard, Jr., made a fifteen-minute suborbital flight aboard *Freedom 7*. In February 1962, astronaut John H. Glenn, Jr., orbited the earth three times aboard *Friendship 7*. But by this time, the Russians were making much longer space flights. In June 1963, Soviet cosmonaut Valeri F. Bykovsky stayed in space for almost five days (June 14–June 19), orbiting the earth eighty-one times. That same month, Valentina V. Tereshkova, another Russian, became the first woman in space.

In March 1965, Soviet cosmonaut Alexei Leonov became the first person to walk in space, protected only by his space suit. He floated about, attached to his space capsule by a fifteen-foot cord. In June 1965, Edward H. White, Jr., orbiting the earth aboard *Gemini 4*, became the first American to walk in space.

The space race could be dangerous. This became all too clear in January 1967 when three American astronauts—Roger B. Chaffee, Gus Grissom, and Ed White—were burned to death. They were trapped inside the *Apollo 1* command module when a fire broke out as the spacecraft was undergoing tests on the ground. And in April of that year, Soviet cosmonaut Valentin M.

The 1960s were a period of severe tension between the two Cold War superpowers—the United States and the Soviet Union. This tension led to dramatic technological achievements, both in weaponry and in space exploration. In 1961, Soviet cosmonaut Yuri Gagarin (opposite) became the first human being in space.

Although the Soviets had made some great strides by putting Yuri Gagarin in space first, the United States made the most impressive achievement of the decade when astronauts Neil Armstrong, Michael Collins, and Edwin "Buzz" Aldrin (above) landed on the moon in July 1969. Placing an American flag on the surface of the moon (opposite), the astronauts not only made history but also captured the imagination of the American people.

Komarov was killed when his *Soyuz 1* spacecraft crashed during its eighteenth orbit around Earth.

By 1969, the United States had pulled ahead in the space race. In December 1968, astronauts Frank Borman, James A. Lovell, Jr., and William A. Anders, aboard *Apollo 8*, had become the first humans to fly around the moon. On July 16, 1969, astronauts Neil Armstrong, Buzz Aldrin, and Michael Collins took off for the moon aboard *Apollo 11*. On July 20, *Apollo 11* was in orbit around the moon. Armstrong and Aldrin crept into the lunar module, *Eagle*, which then separated itself from *Columbia*, the command module, and landed on the moon. "The *Eagle* has landed," announced Armstrong. Four hours later, Armstrong was first to step out onto the lunar surface. "That's one small step for man, one giant leap for mankind," he said to the millions of people on

Earth watching history being made on their TV sets. Armstrong and Aldrin planted an American flag on the moon and then returned safely to Earth. The space race was over.

Organ Transplants

Scientists in the 1960s learned more about the functioning of the human immune system. This allowed surgeons to attempt organ transplants that previously would have been impossible because of the body's natural tendency to reject foreign tissue. In the early 1960s, transplants of the liver and lung were performed. Although the patients died within a few weeks, the procedures raised hopes for greater success in the future.

In 1967, Dr. Christiaan Barnard in South Africa carried out the world's first successful heart transplant. After a five-hour operation, the transplanted heart was beating in the patient's

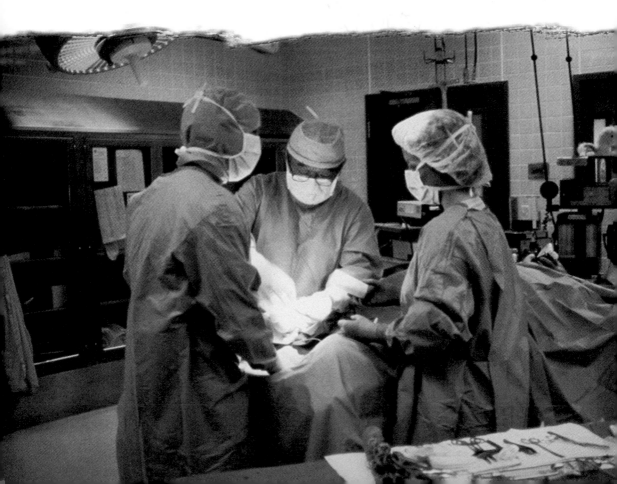

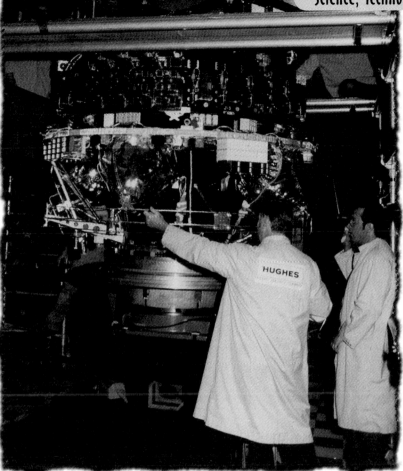

Before the 1960s, a person diagnosed with a diseased heart or other organ often had little hope of survival. That changed in 1967 when the first successful heart transplant was carried out. Although the operation was still dangerous, transplants (opposite, at bottom) offered people with medical problems new hope for the future.

Telstar (left) was the first communications satellite. Seen here in later years after several improvements, Telstar was one of the first steps on the road to the Information Age.

body. The patient lived for eighteen days before dying from lung complications. Almost one hundred heart transplants were performed during the following year.

Telstar

In 1962, AT&T brought science fiction to reality. The company put *Telstar*, the world's first communications satellite, into orbit around the earth. It would use solar power to take TV signals, amplify them, and send them back to Earth. For the first time, Americans could see images that came directly from Europe, and vice versa. *Telstar* could also handle telephone signals, which would help increase person-to-person communications all over the world.

57

An Amazing Decade

The 1960s were marked by incredible changes in American life. With the election of President John F. Kennedy, the United States was hopeful about the future. Beach movies, the Beatles, and new fashion trends gave Americans something to smile about. Soon that would all change.

By the late 1960s, the Vietnam War and civil rights movement had drastically altered the United States. As the war dragged on, some people turned against the government. Others dressed in strange new styles and experimented with drugs and sex. Racial violence caused fear and rioting in many cities. By the end of the decade, Americans seemed to be divided on so many issues that there was little holding society together.

Today, the days of Woodstock and folk music, free love and flower power, are remembered with both fondness and controversy. The 1960s made an enormous impact on America and will most likely continue to be controversial for years to come.

While Americans in the early 1960s looked forward to a bright future, Communist and non-Communist nations in Europe struggled for control of territory. The Berlin Wall (opposite), which went up virtually overnight in August 1961, became a symbol of the strong divisions between democratic and Communist forms of government.

In the United States, a wall of tension also separated the races. Even after the removal of segregation laws, some places refused to allow the races to interact. Alabama Governor George Wallace (below, at left, blocking the door to the University of Alabama in 1963 to prevent black students from entering) was a symbol of the racial tensions and violent racism that the civil rights movements worked to overcome.

1960—Kennedy-Nixon debates are televised; John F. Kennedy is elected president; Chubby Checker (left) and his song "The Twist" start a new dance craze.

1961—President John F. Kennedy is inaugurated; CORE organizes Freedom Rides; Bob Dylan (left) begins singing in New York coffeehouses; New York Yankee Roger Maris hits a then-record 61 home runs; Bay of Pigs invasion fails; President Kennedy sends aid to South Vietnam; Yuri Gagarin becomes the first human being in space.

1962—African-American student James Meredith leads the integration of the University of Mississippi; Wilt Chamberlain scores a record 100 points for the Philadelphia 76ers; Cuban Missile Crisis takes place; AT&T launches *Telstar*; Rachel Carson publishes *Silent Spring*.

1963—SNCC begins program to register black voters in Mississippi; Peter, Paul and Mary release Bob Dylan's "Blowin' in the Wind"; President Kennedy is assassinated in Dallas, Texas; Lyndon B. Johnson (left) becomes president.

1964—Dr. Martin Luther King, Jr., wins the Nobel Peace Prize; The Beatles appear on *The Ed Sullivan Show*, starting the Beatlemania craze; Civil Rights Act is passed; Johnson announces a War on Poverty; Johnson is elected president; Congress passes the Gulf of Tonkin Resolution; President Johnson escalates the war in Vietnam.

1965—Dr. Martin Luther King, Jr., leads a march of Freedom Riders from Selma to Montgomery, Alabama; Racial riots break out in cities around the United States; Malcolm X (left) is assassinated; Voting

Rights Act of 1965 passed; The Barbie doll makes $97 million for Mattel; Cosmonaut Alexei Leonov takes first space walk; Congress passes an antipollution bill to set automobile emission standards.

1966— NOW is formed by Betty Friedan and others; Jacqueline Kennedy (top right) appears in public wearing a miniskirt, indicating that the mini has become high fashion; Black Panther party, founded by Huey Newton (right) and Bobby Seale, is formed.

1967— Summer of Love takes place; Fifty thousand antiwar protesters march on the Pentagon in October; Thurgood Marshall becomes the first black Supreme Court justice; Six-Day War takes place in the Middle East; *Apollo 1* disaster occurs, taking the lives of astronauts Roger Chaffee, Gus Grissom, and Ed White; Dr. Christiaan Barnard performs the first successful heart transplant; Congress passes the Air Quality Act.

1968—Dr. Martin Luther King, Jr., is assassinated in April; Senator Robert F. Kennedy is assassinated in June; Shirley Chisholm (right) becomes the first black woman elected to Congress; Bob Beamon sets a long-jump record in the Olympics; Antiwar demonstrators clash with police at the Democratic National Convention in Chicago; Richard Nixon is elected president; Astronauts Frank Borman, James Lovell, Jr., and William Anders become the first humans to orbit the moon.

1969— New York Jets win Super Bowl III; Woodstock Music and Art Fair takes place; The Weathermen, a more militant offshoot of SDS, is formed to protest the Vietnam War; Astronauts Neil Armstrong (right) and Buzz Aldrin walk on the moon; New York Mets beat the Orioles in the World Series; Oil slick threatens beaches at Santa Barbara, California.

Further Reading

Books

Evans, Harold. *The American Century*. New York: Alfred A. Knopf, 1998.

Holland, Gini. *The 1960's*. San Diego, Calif.: Lucent Books, 1998.

Hurley, Jennifer A. *1960s*. San Diego, Calif.: Greenhaven Press, 2000.

Jennings, Peter, and Todd Brewster. *The Century*. New York: Doubleday, 1998.

Junior Chronicle of the 20th Century. New York: DK Publishing, 1997.

McCormick, Anita Louise. *The Vietnam Antiwar Movement in American History*. Berkeley Heights, N.J.: Enslow Publishers, Inc., 2000.

Schuman, Michael. *Lyndon B. Johnson*. Springfield, N.J.: Enslow Publishers, Inc., 1998.

Spies, Karen Bornemann. *John F. Kennedy*. Berkeley Heights, N.J.: Enslow Publishers, Inc., 1999.

Internet Addresses

The National Civil Rights Museum. 1998. <http://www.midsouth.rr.com/civilrights/> (January 28, 2000).

The Sixties Project. January 28, 1999. <http://lists.village.virginia.edu/sixties/> (January 28, 2000).

White House Historical Association. "John F. Kennedy: Thirty-fifth President, 1961–1963." *The Presidents*. n.d. <http://www.whitehouse.gov/WH/glimpse/presidents/html/jk35.html> (January 28, 2000).

Woodstock: The Music Festival Home Page. October 20, 1996. <http://www.geocities.com/SunsetStrip/3869/woodstock.htm> (January 28, 2000).